CORFU'S SEA
A Nautical P...

By Rodney Agar

CONTENTS

'there is no advantage in living on an island unless you control the waters that wash its shores'

King Alfred the Great

ACKNOWLEDGMENTS

This work is a tribute to the people of the Island of Corfu and its Maritime Heritage. In it I have attempted to highlight the pivotal role which Corfu played as a small island in the Mediterranean, while various Empires strove to push east into the Levant. Necessarily this work describes in more detail events of the 19th and 20th centuries where more records are available. The views expressed are those of my own. I wish to thank and acknowledge, with gratitude, the friends and my family who have helped and given me encouragement with this Nautical Profile of Corfu, especially:

Vasillis Mouhas, and Andreas Papadatos, Library Director, and members of The Reading Society of Corfu who have provided generous support with historical accuracy and illustrations from their library;

The Royal Naval Historical Branch for facts on 'The Corfu Incident';

Murray Johnstone, for assistance during the development of the work; Angela Papageorgiou, Caroline Agar, Diana Manessi, Philip and Valerie Samoylis for their helpful advice.

And last but not least my wife Cecily for her support and 'forebearance amidst the froth' in the writing of the work.

R.S.A

Battleships of the British Mediterranean Fleet
at anchor in Corfu during a goodwill visit in 1912

MAPS

MAP SHOWING SITES OF PRINCIPAL
NAVAL BATTLES IN THE LEVANT

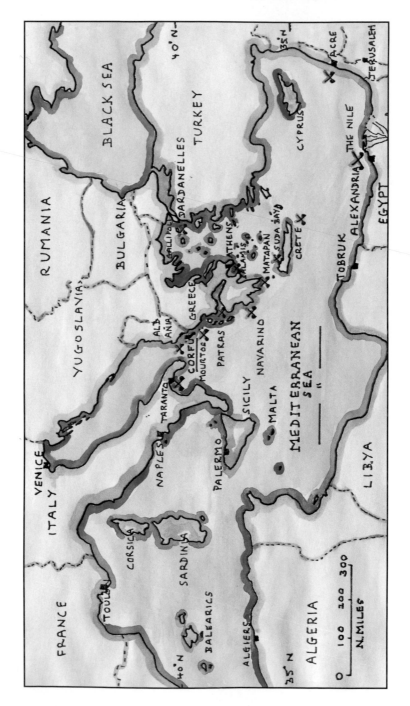

CHAPTER 1

EARLY SEA LEGENDS

Old Men: 'We once were young and brave and strong'
Young men: 'And we're so now, come on and try'
Boys: 'But we'll be strongest bye and bye'

Due place should be given to the youthful chorus

(Sung at The Olympic games in Greece)

EARLY SEA LEGENDS

K erkyra (Corfu) has played a central part in the Maritime History of the Mediterranean for as long as mankind can recall. In ancient days, the island was occupied in turn by Corinthians, Spartans, Athenians and Macedonians. The islands of Corfu and Cephalonia were described as 'the richest prizes in the Ionian' and their people, down the generations, would have been natural sailors. The first naval battles in Greek history were reputedly fought in the Straits of Corfu, when in 655 BC and again in 433 BC, off Mourtos, the Corcyreans rebelled and defeated the Corinthians who had colonised the island.

MAPS OF CORFU AND THE NORTH IONIAN SEA AT THE BATTLE OF SYVOTA. CIRCA 433BC. ONE OF THE EARLIEST KNOWN SEA BATTLES OFF CORFU.

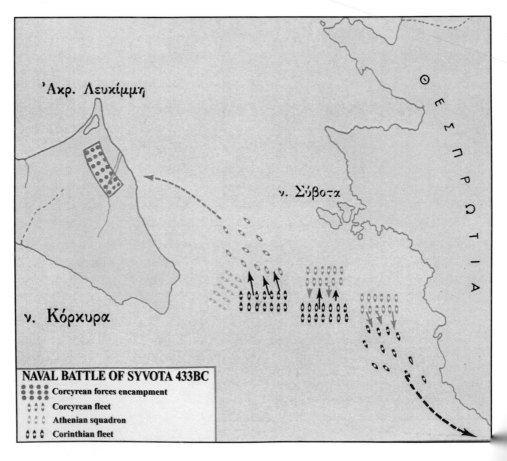

'Ακρ. Λευκίμμη

ν. Σύβοτα

ν. Κόρκυρα

ΘΕΣΠΡΩΤΙΑ

NAVAL BATTLE OF SYVOTA 433BC
Corcyrean forces encampment
Corcyrean fleet
Athenian squadron
Corinthian fleet

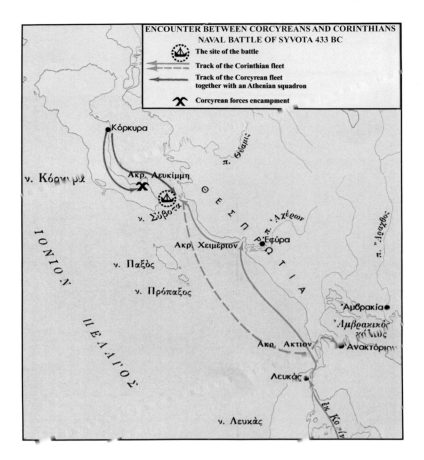

ENCOUNTER BETWEEN CORCYREANS AND CORINTHIANS
NAVAL BATTLE OF SYVOTA 433 BC

The site of the battle
Track of the Corinthian fleet
Track of the Corcyrean fleet together with an Athenian squadron
Corcyrean forces encampment

The Corcyreans then built up a fleet of over 100 ships which took part in the Peloponnesian wars of the 5th century BC. Attempts to recapture Corfu by Greece and her satellites were repeatedly defeated by the Corcyreans.

During this period a deadly naval ship of war, the Trireme - powered by 170 oarsmen with a metal prow for ramming - had been developed and built in Greece and her satellites, including Corfu. The Athenian triremes under Themistocles, at the battle of Salamis, soundly defeated the Persian invasion of Athens, an early example of a land campaign destroyed by a sea battle. Naval conflict played a prominent part in the early life of Corfu, continuously raided by enemies and pirates and racked by civil wars between Athens and its Greek colonies.

Off Preveza, 40 miles south east from Corfu, the Battle of Actium was fought between two Roman fleets in the year 31 BC. The ships taking part were mostly triremes and this was the decisive battle of the Roman civil war. Octavius Augustus, governor of Western Rome defeated Mark Anthony, governor of Rome's Eastern empire. Anthony fled from the battle with Cleopatra to Egypt where they both later committed suicide and Octavius became Caesar to rule the Roman Empire.

Also, part of the folklore, is that after the Trojan wars and at the end of his wanderings Odysseus was shipwrecked and put ashore on Corfu, at Ermones in the Northwest corner. His state of undress favourably surprised the beautiful Princess Nausicaa! Although she wished to marry him, Odysseus's wanderings were over, and he finally sailed for the last time back to his home in Ithaca.

400 YEAR VENETIAN OCCUPATION

Later, Empires looking East used Corfu as a stepping stone for expansion. Firstly the Romans; then 100 years rule by the Angevins from Naples; followed by the 400 year Venetian Occupation from 1386 - 1797. During this period under Venetian Governance the island fiercely resisted numerous sieges from the Turks. In the battle of Lepanto in 1571, fought off Patras at the entrance to the Gulf of Corinth and won by Don Juan of Austria over the Turks, 1,500 Corfiot sailors took part.

A typical ancient Greek Trireme of the time of the Peloponnesian wars of 500 B.C. Powered by 170 oarsmen in three banks. Note the deadly ram at the bows. *

An example of a Lateen Trading Vessel. Circa 500 BC. *

Again, in 1716, Corfu fought off the naval and military power of Turkey whose army had arrived with 60 ships of war to besiege the island. 30,000 Turkish soldiers were landed at Gouvia and the island ravaged, but they failed to take the fortress. Relief occurred with the arrival of the Venetian fleet and the Turks retreated.

The island's strong Venetian shield had provided it with stability and security - 'Venice sat in state, throned on her hundred isles'. Cypress trees were planted and grown to provide masts and spars for the Venetian fleets. Pilgrim galleys would row down the Adriatic calling at Brindisi and Corfu for stores and water as part of the ebb and flow of sea trade through to the Levant. Throughout this period mainland Greece remained a collection of separate states, occupied and ruled by Turkey for centuries who never succeeded in conquering Corfu.

Another example of a Lateen Galley. Circa 500 BC. *

The Venetian dynasty came to an end in 1797 when it was replaced by the French who, under Napoleon , had defeated Venice. The first French occupation lasted only two years, being driven out by a mixed Russian/allied force, but the island was given back to France in 1807 at the Treaty of Tilsit. The main French influence is to be seen in the arcaded buildings on the 'Platea' and a regular street plan in the town. Then, in 1814, Napoleon was defeated at Liepzig and abdicated and Corfu was given up to the British - under whose governance the island achieved Independence and Union with Greece 50 years later in 1864.

Mainly peaceful years followed during the remainder of the 19th and early 20th centuries, until the carnage of World War II, when Corfu was occupied in 1941 for three years by Italy and Germany. By 1945, the island was free again and the second half of the 20th century saw 50 years of peace. Trade and tourism in the island's natural harbours expanded fast. The Balkan eruptions of the 1990's so far have barely touched Corfu whose island sanctuary is now used by NATO forces in the Adriatic. By the start of the 21st century, Corfu's sea legends thus spanned three millenia of nautical history.

CHAPTER 2

CORFU'S STRATEGIC IMPORTANCE

Corfu: 'A jewel set in a Golden sea'

CORFU'S STRATEGIC IMPORTANCE

The fortress over the Corfu strait looking north up the Corfu Channel. 1998.

Huge fortresses built against siege and invasion, first by the Romans in Kassiopi and later the Venetians in Corfu town, bear testimony to the strategic importance of the island -guarding as it does the entrance to the Adriatic.

Geographically Corfu is almost at the central point of the Mediterranean - 450 miles each from Venice in the North and Tripoli to the south - and almost 700 miles equidistant East and West from Alexandria to Algiers. As the prevailing winds come mostly from the Northerly quadrant, Corfu lay astride and to windward of the sailing routes between the Levant and West Mediterranean. Vessels bound North into the Adriatic found the high mountains on the island a notable landmark and it was customary for their masters to try and sight Corfu island for safe navigation on their way.

The safe harbours and anchorages on the Eastern side of the island have enabled Corfu to become a focal point for shipping. Both Nelson and Napoleon in their day considered Corfu to be on a par with Malta as a secure base for the central Mediterranean.

Corfu's strategic importance to the Adriatic and Levant was underlined by the long Venetian occupation. After Venice was defeated by the French in 1797, two notable campaigns, which saw history turned upside down in the Levant, relate to Corfu and the Peloponnese. Firstly, failure by the French to use Corfu in 1798 which they had occupied, lost Napoleon his fleet at the Nile and his Egyptian Expedition was doomed - and with it went French plans for domination of the Middle East and in India. Secondly, the great battle of Navarino in 1827 saw the destruction of the Turco/Egyptian fleet, cutting off the Turkish army and thus securing Independence for Greece. Both related to the strategic importance of Corfu and the Ionian islands.

More recently in the 20th century, World War II again highlighted the strategic importance of the sea basin in the Eastern Mediterranean where control of those waters was vital to the land campaigns of North Africa. British sea control in 1941 brought Italy so near to collapse and loss of her East African Empire, that Germany was forced to intervene to save her ally. The arrival of German bombers and submarines reversed the tide.

Italy and Germany had seen the necessity to occupy Greece in their plans to capture the essential Middle East oil. Corfu, bombed from the air but spared from the land fighting, became a pivotal port on the supply routes to Africa in 1942. However, the British slowly regained sea control, with Malta undefeated, and Germany's 'Afrika Corps' was starved of support and doomed. Thus Hitler's plans, similar to Napoleon's dream before him, to dominate the route to the oil wells of Iraq and Iran were thwarted. In 1943 Italy was invaded and collapsed. The total German withdrawal from Greece took place a year later and Corfu was freed again. Her Island position then enabled her to escape the worst of the 1947 Greek civil war with its threat of Communist domination. World War II once more had proved the strategic importance of the waters around Corfu.

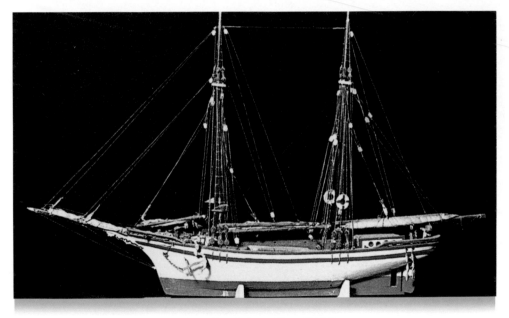

A trading Caique. Circa 1900.*

The Barometer
Long foretold, long last. Short notice, soon past
Quick rise after low, Sure sign of stronger blow
When the glass falls low, Prepare for a blow
When it slowly rises high, Lofty canvas you may fly
At sea with low and falling glass, Soundly sleeps a careless ass.
Only when its high and rising, Truly rests a careful wise one!

CHAPTER 3

19TH CENTURY

'Free and Independent'

19TH CENTURY

The turn of the nineteenth century saw a period of great turbulence for the island during the Napoleonic wars. In 1797 the French defeated the Venetian Republic and occupied Corfu, replacing the historic and influential Venetian governance which had lasted for 400 years.

NELSON AND NAPOLEON

Corfu's pivotal position now formed an historic part in both Nelson's and Napoleon's thoughts and had the island been used by the French fleet escorting Napoleon's Egyptian expedition, history might have taken a different course. However, one year later in 1798, the British under Admiral Nelson destroyed the French fleet at Aboukir Bay where the French had anchored, known as the Battle of the Nile. Napoleon's dream of an invasion into Egypt, Syria and Turkey was destroyed at a stroke, and he was cut off from all communication with France. When we consider his army numbered 40,000 men and had been shipped in 400 transports, escorted by 13 ships of the line and 14 frigates, this was an irreparable catastrophe for France.

THE TRACKS OF NAPOLEON'S AND NELSON'S FLEETS 19TH MAY
- 1ST AUGUST 1798 ENDING AT THE BATTLE OF THE NILE.
NAPOLEON HAD ORDERED THE FRENCH FLEET TO SAIL FOR CORFU BUT THIS
ORDER UNACCOUNTABLY WAS NOT RECEIVED.

During the chase of Napoleon's Egyptian armada by the British fleet Nelson was worried that Napoleon would make for the shelter of Malta or Corfu - a recurring theme in his letters. However the French Admiral Brueys had been unable to sail his ships from Egypt to Corfu, although this was Napoleon's wish, because they had insufficient stores for the passage. After a series of defeats at the hands of the Turks and discontent arising throughout his army, Napoleon returned home to France ignominiously aboard a French frigate, hugging the African shore to escape the British fleet.

The next year, in 1799, Britain was joined by Austria and Russia, and an allied Russian naval squadron captured Corfu from the French. Nelson then considered making the island his Mediterranean base for the British fleet instead of Palermo in Sicily. However he decided against Corfu where he thought the Russian admiral "a Blackguard"! - and remained at Palermo, where the presence of his mistress Lady Hamilton nearer at Naples also helped sway the issue.

In 1807 Corfu was returned again to the French at the Treaty of Tilsit, but this was short-lived. In 1814, after Napoleon's abdication, the island was reoccupied by the British. Corfu then became the capital of the Ionian Republic when, in 1815 at the Treaty of Paris, the Ionian Islands were made a free and independent state under the sole protection of Britain.

The 'Victory' - a 100 gun Ship of the Line

17

IONIAN REPUBLIC

After 1815 a period of stability then followed for 50 years under British governance. Corfu was described as 'the finest harbour and strongest fortress in the Adriatic' and the Ionian Islands traded under their own flag - with a small union jack in the corner as a symbol of protection against piracy. The Barbary pirates from Algiers ranged far into the Eastern Mediterranean, landing on beaches on the Ionian Islands to raid and capture what they could find. Villages near the shore came to be built on hilltops for protection.

Gradually British rule reverted to a greater proportion of self government. Together with its newfound freedom, order, prosperity, and education followed. Roads, harbours and quays encouraged a vigorous growth of maritime trade. Even the game of cricket was introduced by successive British garrisons! Ginger beer in stone bottles followed after the game to quench thirsts - a legacy which continues to the present day.

Although Corfu and the Ionian Islands had become independent under British Governance during this early nineteenth century period, Greece itself was still ruled by Turkey and Egypt and was fighting a war of Independence. In 1826, the various Greek factions achieved unity and elected as the first President of Greece a Corfiot - Count Capodistrias. The Anglo-Hellenic relationship was forged when Capodistrias installed a British Naval officer (Lord Cochrane) as First Admiral of Greece to fight the Turks and Egyptians until they were cleared from Greece. Separately, an alliance of Britain, France and Russia signed a protocol which guaranteed the right of Greece to independence and pledged military assistance - an army provided by France and a naval force from Britain and Russia.

The Winds of Corfu
North -   Boreas or Meltemi
North East - Gregale
South East - Scirocco
North West - Maestro

BATTLE OF NAVARINO

This support culminated in the Battle of Navarino in October 1827 in the Greek Peloponnese where the British and their allies won a major naval victory over the Turco-Egyptian fleet. A combined allied fleet of 25 ships led by the British Mediterranean commander (Admiral Codrington) annihilated a large Turco-Egyptian fleet of 82 ships under the Egyptian Bey Ibrahim in the Bay of Navarino, sinking 55 of their ships. A Turkish army of 20,000 soldiers on shore watched but were helpless to intervene. This was the last ever major sea battle to be fought between fleets under sail only.

THE BATTLE OF NAVARINO OCTOBER 1827

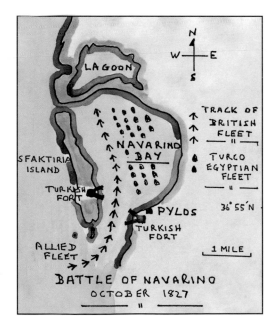

This victory had similar features to that of the Nile where both the vanquished forces were moored in a supposedly safe anchorage unable to manoeuvre. Defeat of their fleet virtually destroyed the Turco-Egyptian ability to maintain and conduct further land operations on mainland Greece. These two naval battles, namely the Nile and Navarino, highlight how two major land campaigns were destroyed by the related sea actions, in both cases cutting of all communication with their supporting powers.

UNION WITH GREECE

A year after Navarino in 1828, the Turkish army was expelled from mainland Greece by a French/Greek force. Greece was at last freed from Turkish rule for all time and achieved unified Independence under President Capodistrias. In Corfu, already independent as the capital of the satellite Ionian Republic, Greek superseded Italian as the official language in 1852. Finally, the steady demand for union with the mother country resulted in the Ionian Islands being fully reconstituted as part of Greece at the Treaty of London in 1864.

The last British High Commissioner left in HMS MARLBOROUGH and the Greek flag was hoisted on 2nd June 1864. Four days later, this landmark event was celebrated when King George I of the Hellenes steamed to Corfu from Navarino in his frigate HELLAS at the head of an international naval squadron. He landed at the citadel to a gun salute and received the keys of the town. The ceremony was sealed with pealing church bells and a service in the church of St. Spiridion, Patron Saint of Corfu.

The Battle of Navarino in 1827. The last major sea battle fought by ships under sail only. A Turkish/Egyptian Fleet of 87 ships was destroyed by a British led allied fleet of 28 ships. This action led to the defeat of the Turkish land campaign and independence for Greece. The Turkish fort can be seen in the left foreground on SFAKTIRIA Island. *

CHAPTER 4

EARLY 20TH CENTURY

'Tranquil Years'

EARLY 20TH CENTURY

After union with Greece, some peaceful years came to Corfu until the two world wars of the 20th century broke this tranquillity. Corfu came to be visited frequently by naval squadrons from various nations for recreation and goodwill. Pictures of lines of battleships anchored in the roads off Corfu town and other naval visits throughout the century bear testimony to its security as a safe anchorage. The recent extension of the new port where large cruise liners now berth safely adds to Corfu's sea legend and the island became an integral part of many Mediterranean cruises.

CORFU AT PEACE

In 1916, during World War 1, the island was used by the allies but suffered little by all accounts except for some severe shortages of food. The advent of steam and propeller driven ships had displaced Corfu's previous advantage of a windward position. The large natural anchorage at Milos in the Aegean became the principal British base for the Dardanelles campaign against Turkey- Churchill's disastrous 'Balkan Enterprise'.

'Kouloura' on the North East Coast of Corfu. This famous house looks out over the North Corfu channel. It belonged formerly to the late Commander Disney Vaughan-Hughes, Royal Navy, and his family over several generations.

After the peace of 1918, Corfu enjoyed respite from foreign occupation though disturbed for a short while by being bombarded by an Italian naval squadron in 1923 over a dispute. This occurred when an Italian general was murdered by brigands on the mainland. Italy asked Greece for compensation, and then landed troops and occupied Corfu for two months as 'security'. The dispute was resolved when the League of Nations intervened and Italy withdrew. The ill fated Greek-Turkish war of 1922, started by Greece but in which Kemal Ataturk retook Asia Minor for Turkey, left Corfu unscathed.

Battleships at anchor in Corfu Harbour circa 1900. *

Britain had developed Malta as an island naval base and there are many instances of visits by the British Mediterranean Fleet to Corfu, a very popular island anchorage. Typical local hospitality during calls ashore and after speeches would be a tea party and dancing - longlasting - consisting of brandy, tea, grapes and a cake tasting strongly of Ouzo! The mainland shore opposite Corfu near Mourtos became sought after for shooting parties from visiting warships and schooners from the North. Partridge, quail, woodcock and duck were the game birds on the receiving end of intrepid 'guns' landing for sport and exercise.

Ships of the British Mediterranean Fleet anchored in Corfu Harbour. Circa 1912.*
(HMS RENOWN on the right. Two ROYAL SOVEREIGN class battleships in the centre)

PRINCE PHILIP OF GREECE

Corfu had become a fashionable Mediterranean resort where Kaiser William II of Germany and others had summer palaces and retreats. The Greek Royal family also had bought a property in Corfu as their summer residence - Villa 'Mon Repos' - just south of Corfu town. This house overlooking the sea had been built for and used by the High Commissioner during the British Protectorate of the Ionian Islands in the previous century. In 1903, Prince Andrew, the younger brother of King Constantine 1 of Greece, had married Princess Alice of Battenberg, sister of Lord Louis Mountbatten. Here in Corfu,. at Villa 'Mon Repos', Princess Alice gave birth to a baby boy called Philip on 10th June 1921.

The early 1920's saw turbulent days and in 1922 the Greek Monarchy was overthrown by a revolutionary coup as a result of the defeat of the Greek army by the Turks in Asia Minor. King Constantine I abdicated. Prince Andrew of Greece, the baby Prince Philip's father and a Lieutenant General in the Greek Army, was tried as a scapegoat and condemned to death, but the sentence was later commuted to banishment for life. In December 1922, he and Princess Alice departed from Athens aboard the British cruiser HMS CALYPSO for Corfu, where they loved to stay, to collect the rest of their family including the young Prince Philip before sailing away from Greece into exile. The Greek Monarchy was not restored until King George II returned to Greece in 1935.

After being educated in Britain, Prince Philip of Greece was commissioned into the British Royal Navy in which he served with distinction for 13 years during World War II and afterwards, including the Battle of Matapan off the southern Peloponnese. After the war he changed his name to Mountbatten. In 1947 he married the then Princess Elizabeth, later to be crowned Queen Elizabeth II of Great Britain, and became The Duke of Edinburgh.

Fishermen handling their nets off the twin forts of Corfu. Circa 1900. *

HMS HOOD

In July 1938, a British naval visit took place when Vice Admiral Sir Andrew Cunningham went to Corfu in the battlecruiser HMS HOOD, with HMS REPULSE in company. Both these fine ships were sunk later in World War II. His Majesty the King of Greece was in residence and, after the usual calls, inspected and dined in HMS HOOD before watching the cinema and staying until 2.am! He struck Admiral Cunningham as 'a solemn and serious-minded man'. This meeting would stand both of them in good stead later in 1941, when Admiral Cunningham was Commander of the British Mediterranean Fleet carrying out firstly the support and then the evacuation of Greece by allied troops.

The Battlecruiser HMS Hood off Corfu in July 1938 as she passed HMS Repulse.
The Hood, wearing the flag of Admiral Sir Andrew Cunningham, was visited by
HM the King of the Hellenes in Corfu who dined on board, thus forging their relationship. +

The Moon
A Full moon, rising clear, foretells fair
A Pale moon doth rain
A Halo round the moon, rain cometh soon
A Red Moon doth blow
A White moon doth neither rain nor snow

CHAPTER 5

WORLD WAR II

'Dominant air supremacy'

WORLD WAR II

Corfu suffered dreadfully in the second world war. In 1940 Italy, under Mussolini, joined the 'Axis' alliance with Germany in the age old dance looking Eastwards. The strategic need for the oil wells of the Middle East pointed to the route through Greece. Italy sought to conquer Corfu and the Ionian Islands, then Salonica and southwards and gave an ultimatum to surrender. Greece rejected this and was invaded in an unprovoked assault by Italy via Albania on 28th October 1940.

INVASION OF GREECE AND OCCUPATION OF CORFU

The Italian invasion of Greece was driven back by the Greek Army who advanced 30 miles into Albania, and this campaign stagnated into the winter of 1940 without change. At sea, the Italian Navy was preparing to attack and annexe Corfu. However before they were able to, the British crippled the Italian battlefleet at Taranto on 11th November 1940 by an imaginative and daring attack by British Carrier borne aircraft, in which three Italian battleships and two cruisers were sunk. Italian Naval morale, already on the wane due to lack of aggressive action, was dented even further and Italian warships were moved to bases further away. Other related sea actions also took place against the Italian Navy, when Greek destroyers, based in Patras in the Gulf of Corinth, attacked Taranto. Greek submarines patrolled defensively off the north coast of Corfu which was spared attack until the Germans joined Italy's aggression in April 1941.

Admiral Sir Andrew Cunningham KCB, C-in-C of the British Mediterranean Fleet during the invasion and evacuation of Greece in 1941, when the Italians took possession of Corfu.+

The Aircraft Carrier HMS Illustrious and her escort preparing for the Fleet Air Arm raid on the Italian Battlefleet at Taranto in November 1940. This raid, where 3 Italian Battleships were sunk, forestalled the Italian Naval attack on Corfu.+

The Italian/German invasion of Greece presaged another chapter in the strong Anglo- Hellenic relationship when Britain undertook to honour the 1939 guarantee of assistance to Greece. The British King George V signalled to the King of the Hellenes: 'Your cause is our cause; we shall be fighting against a common foe.' A British and Commonwealth Expeditionary force of 40,000 troops lightly equipped was hastily prepared and sent to Greece from Africa but this was to no avail. On 6th April 1941, Germany joined the Italian aggression and invaded Greece through Bulgaria. For the vital sea links of the Levant the danger from Italian highlevel bombing was now augmented by the accurate and deadly dive bombing from German Stukas.

The German 12th Army consisting of 17 divisions swept down through Greece to the Peloponnese, with overwhelming air support and over-ran a Greek Army exhausted by five months winter campaigning. The superior numbers of the German Air Force dominated the skies and German parachutists captured many islands and airfields to control the Aegean. The British Navy, involving four cruisers, 23 destroyers and 18 merchantmen, lost many ships in supporting and evacuating over 50,000 allied troops.

THE GERMAN INVASION 1941

On 28th April 1941 Greece surrendered and the King evacuated first to Crete then on 23rd May to Egypt in the destroyer HMS DEFENDER. Corfu once again became the object of ravage, bombing, invasion and fierce fighting ashore. Much of Corfu town was destroyed by bombing and occupied by the Italians, whose garrison eventually by 1943 numbered nearly 7,000 men. A poignant story tells of the entry of the Germans into Athens on 27th April 1941, when a message was received in Egypt from the Athens wireless station; 'closing down for the last time, hoping for happier days. God be with you, and for you'. Then silence.

SUBMARINE ATTACK IN CORFU ROADS - MIERS V.C.

Both Italy and Germany used the focal harbour at Corfu to supply and support their Africa Corps offensive against the British in North Africa. In March 1942, Lieutenant ACC Miers, Royal Navy in HM submarine 'TORBAY' entered Corfu Roads at dusk, on the surface, in search of four large German troopships reported there. He had to dive twice to avoid patrol craft, so after charging batteries he went on submerged intending to attack by moonlight

HM Submarine Torbay, in which Lieutenant ACC Miers, RN won the Victoria Cross for entering and sinking two German Supply ships in Corfu Harbour in 1942.+

However, there was no sign of the troopships through his periscope, so he waited until forced to withdraw to avoid being rammed by one of the enemy patrol vessels. Next morning he re- entered Corfu Roads, submerged, in daylight, and torpedoed two large supply ships, sinking one and damaging the other. Although he had spent 17 hours inside Corfu Harbour in the most dangerous conditions and was then hunted by German warships in the clear waters of the Corfu Channel, the TORBAY escaped safely. For this daring exploit Miers was awarded the Victoria Cross, which is the highest British award for fighting personnel showing exceptional courage in the face of the enemy.

Commander A. C. Miers VC, Royal Navy.+

German evacuation of Greece - Civil War

After Italy had surrendered to the Allies in 1943, Germany strengthened its occupation of Greece. Corfu was bombed heavily when the German troops attacked and decimated the Italian garrison - their erstwhile allies. The German occupation created much misery and food became scarce. A ship carrying away some of the Italian garrison was bombed and sunk in the Corfu channel with great loss of life, and a huge area of the town was damaged in the fighting. The church of St. Spiridion, Patron Saint of Corfu, miraculously remained untouched. By the autumn of 1944 the Germans decided to evacuate from the whole of Greece and there then followed the most crucial internal crisis since Greek unification 120 years before.

The complete German withdrawal had left the country in ruins, with roads and railways destroyed. Both the Monarchy and Government suffered popular distrust and civil war now broke out between the bands of partisans, previously armed by Britain to fight the Germans. Greece faced the threat of internal Communist domination by its Marxist led groups ELAS and EAM each seeking power.

Greek Naval Officers decorated for bravery in Alexandra by Admiral Sir John Cunningham KCB, British C-in-C Levant, on behalf of HM the King. (left to right) Commander Matheou DSC, for gallantry during the Greek campaign; Rear Admiral Cavadias KBE; the Crown Prince Paul and Princess Frederica of Greece; Admiral Sir John Cunningham; Lieut. Cdr. Demilatis DSC, for skill and operations commanding the Greek destroyer SPENDONI, Royal Hellenic Navy. 1943+

However across the narrow waters of the Ionian sea, Corfu escaped much of the ravages of this conflict between ELAS and EAM. The German garrison had left the island without any fighting and a British Commando unit was the first to land without opposition as a liberating force.

Then in November 1944, at the request of the Greek Government in exile, a combined British and Greek military force landed to secure Athens, Salonika and Patras. By January 1945 the armed ELAS insurgency in mainland Greece had been defeated. British and Greek troops controlled Attica and the struggle for Athens was over, but at a cost of 1,000 British and many Greek casualties. An all party Regency Government was declared under Archbishop Damaskinos. Greece was spared Communist subjugation and in Churchill's words 'Stood at the nerve-centre of power, law, and freedom in the Western world.' But further up the Adriatic, both Albania and Yugoslavia fell under their partisan's Communist tyranny. Corfu's island position had again given it security.

HMS Corfu. A British armed merchant cruiser was named H.M.S. Corfu after the island, pictured in her war dress after refit in 1943. She was formerly a P&O passenger liner and was used on convoy duties as a troopship. +

*Left to right. Sir Anthony Eden, The Regent of Greece Archbishop Damaskinos,
The Prime Minister of Great Britain Mr. Winston Churchill, in Athens at Christmas 1944
during the all party talks on the future of Greece.* ✠

*British Prime Minister Mr Winston Churchill on board the cruiser HMS Ajax during his visit to
Greece at Christmas 1944. The Ajax at anchor off Athens stood within range of an Elas battery of
77mm guns. On the afternoon of the Prime Minister's arrival one shell fell 200 yards away in the
sea. The preliminary meetings with the Archbishop of Athens were held on board the cruiser.* ✠

CHAPTER 6

THE CORFU INCIDENT

'Albanian ambitions'

THE CORFU INCIDENT

At the end of World War II the Western Allies'advance into Germany met headlong with the Russian armies advancing from the East. The idealogical split between the Allies and Russia started the 'Cold War'which was to last for four decades, with the threat of a Russian frontier spreading down to the Adriatic. The first major clash occurred in 1946 in the Greek Civil War, which was to last for three years. The Communist Greek guerrillas, formerly the defeated ELAS, started an armed terrorist campaign in Northern Greece with Russian and Eastern block support - a war almost as horrific as that against the Nazis. Tangible military support for the guerrillas came from Albania just over the water from Corfu which remained unscathed again after the guerrilla defeat by government forces in 1949.

Huge ferries with goods and tourists now plough a peaceful furrow through the Corfu Channel from the Adriatic to Corfu and mainland Greece - but the scenario might have been otherwise. In 1946 an attempt by Albania to control this busy, narrow waterway was thwarted by Britain in a naval confrontation, with its unexpected and tragic consequences. This action became known as 'The Corfu Incident' and was significant in the wider context of Communist expansion south and the threat to Corfu's security.

The British destroyer H.M.S. Volage in 1945 before being struck by a mine in the North Corfu Channel. This class of destroyer was armed with 4 x 4.5 inch guns and 10 torpedoes. +

THE CORFU INCIDENT

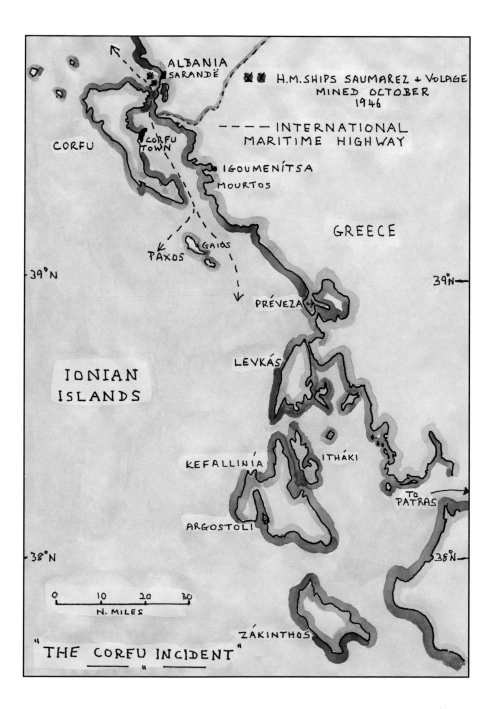

"THE CORFU INCIDENT"

THE 'CORFU INCIDENT'

The North Corfu Channel is part Greek and part Albanian, and an artery for sea traffic between Greece and the Adriatic. The whole Corfu Channel, both North and South, by International Law is an international maritime highway through which merchant and warships of all nations are entitled to exercise the 'right of innocent passage'. It was heavily mined during World War II, but was subsequently cleared by British Royal Navy mineseepers and a swept channel established.

After the defeat of Germany, Albania claimed territorial rights over their part of the North Corfu Channel which threw into question the unfettered right of all shipping to use the channel. In May 1946, two British cruisers, HM Ships ORION and SUPERB, were fired on by Albanian shore batteries as they passed southwards through the channel opposite Kassiopi on a visit to Corfu. No hits were scored. After a strong protest by Britain which Albania rejected it was made clear that if British warships were in future fired on, fire would be returned.

HMS Volage after being mined in 'The Corfu Incident'secured astern of H.M.S. Leander, with her bow blown off by a mine in the North Corfu Channel in October 1946. The bow section sank in the Corfu channel and a new bow was built in Malta.The Volage saw further service. +

HMS Saumarez after being mined by Albania on 22nd October 1946. Astern of her is HMS Volage. Both ships are secured astern off the cruiser HMS Leander. The Saumarez was subsequently scrapped. +

Following the legal wrangling, the British decided to transit the North Corfu Channel again to test Albanian reactions. On 22nd October 1946 a stronger naval force consisting of two cruisers, HM Ships MAURITIUS and LEANDER escorted by two destroyers sailed north from Corfu Port. However, Albania had secretly mined the channel. The two British destroyers, HM Ships SAUMAREZ and VOLAGE, struck mines which exploded under them as they rounded the channel between Albania and NorthEast Corfu. A tense situation developed while a strong northwest wind blew the two badly damaged ships further into the minefield and towards the Albanian shore batteries. However, no gun action ensued and the cruisers in the meantime dared not approach further into the minefield to give assistance due to the high risk of also striking a mine.

The destroyer VOLAGE, although mined herself, managed to get out a towline and slowly towed the SAUMAREZ stern first out of the dangerous minefield back into the channel, securing eventually to the cruiser LEANDER off Corfu Port for firefighting and medical assistance. But the VOLAGE (herself) was so badly damaged that she finally broke her back and the bow half sank. The remains of both ships were towed back to Malta by tug and the VOLAGE was repaired with a new bow. The SAUMAREZ was scrapped. The loss of life was 44 British sailors killed and 42 wounded. Their graves and memorial lie to-day in the peace and tranquillity of the British Cemetery in Corfu town.

A British minesweeper in the North Corfu Channel in November 1946. One of the 9 British minesweepers which were engaged in sweeping the minefield laid in the North Corfu channel in November 1946, after the British destroyers Volage and Saumarez were damaged by hitting mines. The Albanian shore can be seen in the background. The mine just swept in the foreground is a German G Y type.+

ALBANIAN PROTEST

On 30th October the Albanian Government lodged a protest with the United Nations against 'the unauthorised penetration of British warships into Albanian waters'. But despite this, Royal Navy minesweepers re-swept the North Corfu Channel on 13th November. 22 mines were swept up and destroyed, their condition beyond doubt indicating that they had been laid recently, and as the position of the minefield also was closely overlooked by Albanian shore batteries it was clear that the mines had been laid either by the Albanians themselves or with their concurrence. No further action or incidents occurred.

A German G Y type swept up in the North Corfu Channel in November 1946, just off Kassiopi and the Albanian coast after the 'Corfu Incident', being examined by British sailors. It can be seen to be in good state of preservation, recently laid.+

INTERNATIONAL COURT'S DECISION

The British Government placed its case before the Security Council of the United Nations, which concluded that the United Kingdom and Albania should refer the dispute to the International Court of Justice. The Court's findings were that Albania was responsible for the mining of the two destroyers and should pay damages, and that Albanian sovereignty had not been violated by the passage of British warships. With regard to the subsequent minesweeping operations the Court found that'Britain was technically in the wrong in operating in Albanian waters, but that there were extenuating circumstances arising out of Albania's conduct.'Albania's gold reserves were frozen in London but it was not until many years later that the damage compensation was finally paid and the dispute concluded. Meanwhile, extension of Communist control of waters into the North Ionian and West coast of Greece had been checked and ships on lawful passage in the Corfu Channel passed again without hindrance.

For several decades afterwards, searchlights from Albania would sweep their side of the narrow channel all night in a sinister show of defiance, defining the line between freedom and repression. But very few Albanians made their escape across the water from fortress Albania.

HMS Mauritius, the British cruiser that led the fatal force transitting the North Corfu Channel on 22nd October 1946. (Note: The author served as a Midshipman in this ship in 1948)+

CHAPTER 7

LATE 20TH CENTURY

'A small smudge on the horizon slowly became a sharpening outline - which, as we sailed closer, became the green hillsides of Corfu. What Joy!'

LATE 20TH CENTURY

After 1946 peaceful years followed again. The second half of the 20th century saw the growth of a booming tourist industry which brought undreamed of prosperity to Corfu and a sea change from its traditional olive and farming culture.

HMS Glory visits Corfu 1949. A Greek naval motor launch proceeding to the aircraft carrier H.M.S. Glory whilst anchored off Corfu port on a visit to the island in 1949. Corfu's twin fortresses and army barracks in the background.+

TOURISM

The island's central geographical position and its beauty provide a natural background for tourism. 'Glasnost'has loosened the purse strings of East European countries with no seaboard - and Slavs and Russians now swell the numbers of traditional British, Italian, German and Scandinavian visitors.

The 1953 earthquakes which devastated many Ionian islands barely touched Corfu and the constant current flowing through the Corfu Channel keeps its water and beaches uniquely clean for the Mediterranean. Brightly coloured caiques ply their way up and down the harbours and bays. Corfu harbour is full of cruise liners and monster ferries, with rippling bulbous bow-waves, carve their way unimpeded through the Corfu Channel to Italy or the ports of Igonoumetsa and Patras - for centuries the gateway to mainland Greece.

Greek Royal visit to British destroyer off Corfu in 1961. The King and Queen of the Hellenes, accompanied by the Crown Prince Constantine, visiting British warships on a visit to Corfu in July 1961. King Paul, wearing the uniform of Admiral in the Royal Navy, flew his flag in H.M.S. Solebay and is seen here inspecting a royal guard of honour in the destroyer H.M.S. So'ebay (Captain J. Smallwood, Royal Navy).+

NATO AND THE BALKANS

Communism in Eastern Europe and down the east Adriatic Coast finally collapsed in the 'Glasnost' of the 1990's. The Balkans again erupted, when the experiment of a United Yugoslavia fell apart, and NATO and the United Nations intervened to douse the fire of a Balkan conflict. In 1993, Corfu harbour again saw the ensigns of many navies flying from warships at anchor and alongside in the new port - from the huge aircraft carriers of the United States. Britain and France to frigates and destroyers of other NATO forces. The island's secure anchorages again became a base for ships entering the Adriatic on blockade - this time to support the United Nations embargo on Yugoslavia.

Corfu once more found itself having fiercely to guard its shores against the outpouring of migrants and thieves, attempting to break out from the poverty of an Albanian Communist legacy. The age old dance of Balkan religious and ethnic conflict created a refugee problem of unforeseen dimensions. The waters of the Adriatic became an escape route to Italy while Bosnians, Serbs, Kosovas and Albanians all looked to the West for a better life. Mafia undertones fuelled this exodus and the task to monitor and intercept their fast launches, moving at speeds of 30-40knots, became a new priority with matching ships, speed and electronic age techniques.

The narrow passage of the Corfu Channel today is patrolled continuously with success by the Greek Navy and Coastguard. While covetous Albanian eyes view Corfu as a stepping-stone to western prosperity, illegal immigrants are caught at sea or ashore after landing. One such was heard to say, while being deported back to Albania, *'see you again in three days'!* The world will have to show compassion in the rebuilding of a ravaged Balkan infrastructure, so that its peoples, freed from Communism, may create a better life for themselves within.

YACHTSMAN'S JOURNEY IN THE IONIAN

Corfu's prosperity saw the growth of sea traffic together with trade and, in the perfect Ionian waters, a new nautical activity mushroomed - yachting. The safe harbour of Gouvia, just north of Corfu port, is now a major yacht marina, home to many charter yachts and owners who lay up for the winter there, adding to the Sea Legend. The North Ionian Sea and harbours and anchorages on the east coast of Corfu are fast becoming a yachtsman's paradise. From there the Ionian offers a warm and pleasing cruising ground for yachtsmen.

then...1895 A.D

Corfu - The fortress built by the Venetians; the army barracks built by the British; and fishing harbour at Mandraki. Circa 1895.+

now...1995 A.D

The same harbour at Mandraki. Circa 1995, now home of the Corfu Yacht Club.

Yachts racing off Corfu - 1986

Starting from Gouvia, a week's or fortnight's yachting holiday can embrace cruising down into the Southern Ionian Sea calling at Paxos, through the Levkas canal, Cephalonia, Ithaca, Zante and beyond or into the Gulfs of Patras and Corinth. The harbours of Gaios and Fiskardo are among the most picturesque in the world. The delights of Ionian cruising are now legendary and the weather between May and October is warm with gentle breezes. The occasional Scirroco (South wind) or Maestro (North Wind) are moderate to strong but cause only a short sea inside the islands. Light winds or calms occur often in the morning, ensuring a flat blue sea, before rising in the afternoon. Historically, in the days of sail these calms showed the necessity for the oar-powered galley and trireme either to attack or escape.

In the waters off Mourtos at the southern end of Corfu, the yachtsman can envisage where early battles were fought. He can sail southwards to visit the huge bay of Navarino in the south-west Peloponnese, site of the naval victory that brought Independence to Greece. If time permits he may cruise further and visit the magnificent Venetian fortresses at Methoni and Koroni, and onwards to the East and the forbidding Capes of Matapan and Malea. The rock-like headland of Malea rises to 2,000ft and marks the entrance to the Aegean. The waters off Matapan and in the Kithera Channels off Crete saw the fierce sea battles of World War II. Here in 1941, for the first time in history, air power dominated over sea-borne forces and the demise of the line of battleship after three centuries had begun.

Having rounded Cape Malea he can look forward to the Cyclades, sunwashed islands with white villas and the clearest blue water, and Milos, with its huge natural harbour - main base for the allied fleets in the Dardanelles campaign of World War 1. Here in the Aegean he will encounter the Meltemi - strong winds that blow for five days - and savour the delights of fish and birds.

Sunset over Corfu from the fortress

Common Dolphin

Bottlenose Dolphin

Greek waters are famous for Dolphins. There are two main species in the Mediterranean - the common dolphin and bottle-nose dolphin. The former can swim fast at speeds up to 30 knots and, having approached fast from nowhere, often play off a yacht's bows while maintaining station to amuse themselves. Being mammals they breathe as they rise and dip in the waves and their effortless grace never ceases to please the senses. Rarely does one see a shark. Often, a warship's company would bathe over the side safely in mid- Mediterranean. Their protection being a ship's boat, lookout and a sailor armed with a rifle - almost more of a worry than a shark!

1985 Yachts at anchor off Mourtos in the Corfu channel. 'Dozmare', the author's yacht anchored in the foreground

EPILOGUE

Today, tourist brochures extol the virtues of Corfu as an island holiday for its beauty, sunshine and simplicity. The island's irresistible blue sea, its mesmeric views of mountains and greenery, architecture, yachting and sprawling olive groves all make for an idyllic picture. But the 21st century will test the ingenuity of its people in how to match the demands of a tourist industry, bursting forth from its own success, and together retain a compatible island life. The sea change of the last fifty years has created a watershed for 'one of the richest prizes in the Ionian'.

For Corfiotes, an island community, their heritage embraces a far wider culture evolved from centuries of the sea and Byzantine, Neapolitan, Venetian, French and British influence. Their history remains ingrained in the massive walls of the fortresses which protected Corfu town; the safe natural harbours around the coast; and the sea legends and battles fought around their island. After three millenia, the waters that wash its shores will continue to shape and secure Corfu's unique island position at the entrance to the Adriatic.

The Sun
If the sun goes Pale to bed,
Rain tomorrow it is said.
Evening Red, morning Grey,
Help the sailor on his way.

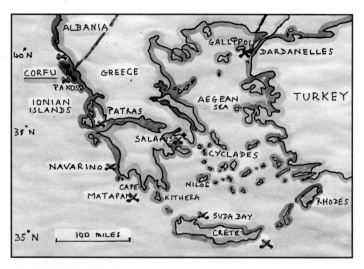

The Currents off Corfu

The Mediterranean Sea, landlocked except for the Strait of Gibraltar, is almost tideless. The currents that flow within it are caused by evaporation whereby the lost water is replaced by inflow, two thirds of which is received from the Atlantic ocean and one third from the surrounding rivers. Circulation of the sea is also created when the water, after evaporation, changes salinity, becomes denser and sinks.

The currents off Corfu are caused mainly by the basin of water circulation at the entrance to the Adriatic which flows anti-clockwise. This basin is the end product of the water inflow from the Atlantic which runs easterly along the North African coast and circles back, eventually, up the West coast of Greece before turning south-west to Italy. Off Corfu, this flow creates an underlying northerly current which is fairly constant and runs at speeds up to 3/4 knot.

In the Corfu Channel itself, fresh water coming from the mountains and mainland mixes with the underlying flow. Here the surface current is mostly southerly, but its strength and direction are also affected by the winds. A strong north wind boosts the southerly flow and a south wind causes a northerly flow, both of which can run at speeds up to 2 knots, with a rise and fall of 2-3 ft. These flowing currents in the waters around Corfu keep the sea very clean - among the best in the Mediterranean.

Ancient seaman's rhyme:

The Sky

A Red sky at night is a sailor's delight
A red sky in the morning is a sailorman's warning
The evening Red and the morning Grey,
Are sure signs of a fine day.
But the evening grey and the morning red,
Makes the sailor shake his head.

Mackerel skies and mare's tails
Tall ships carry low sails.
Clouds like rocks and towers,
Look for squalls and showers

When rain comes before the wind,
Halyards sheets and braces mind,
But when wind comes before rain,
Soon you may make sail again.

If clouds are gathering thick and fast,
Keep sharp lookout for sail and mast,
But if they slowly onward crawl,
Shoot your lines, nets and trawl!